G.O.D.
(Good. Orderly. Direction.)

by Lee Coffey

SAMUEL FRENCH

Copyright © 2022 by Lee Coffey
All Rights Reserved
Cover artwork by Sadhbh McLoughlin

G.O.D. (Good. Orderly. Direction.) is fully protected under the copyright laws of the British Commonwealth, including Canada, the United States of America, and all other countries of the Copyright Union. All rights, including professional and amateur stage productions, recitation, lecturing, public reading, motion picture, radio broadcasting, television, online/digital production, and the rights of translation into foreign languages are strictly reserved.

ISBN 978-0573-13371-8

concordtheatricals.co.uk
concordtheatricals.com

FOR AMATEUR PRODUCTION ENQUIRIES

UNITED KINGDOM AND WORLD
EXCLUDING NORTH AMERICA
licensing@concordtheatricals.co.uk
020-7054-7298

Each title is subject to availability from Concord Theatricals,
depending upon country of performance.

CAUTION: Professional and amateur producers are hereby warned that *G.O.D. (Good. Orderly. Direction.)* is subject to a licensing fee. The purchase, renting, lending or use of this book does not constitute a licence to perform this title(s), which licence must be obtained from the appropriate agent prior to any performance. Performance of this title(s) without a licence is a violation of copyright law and may subject the producer and/or presenter of such performances to penalties. Both amateurs and professionals considering a production are strongly advised to apply to the appropriate agent before starting rehearsals, advertising, or booking a theatre. A licensing fee must be paid whether the title is presented for charity or gain and whether or not admission is charged.

This work is published by Samuel French, an imprint of Concord Theatricals Ltd.

The Professional Rights in this play are controlled by Lisa Richards Creatives, 6 Goodwins Court, St. Martin's Lane, London WC2N 4LL.

No one shall make any changes in this title for the purpose of production. No part of this book may be reproduced, stored in a retrieval system, scanned, uploaded, or transmitted in any form, by any means, now known or yet to be invented, including mechanical, electronic, digital, photocopying, recording, videotaping, or otherwise, without the prior written permission of the publisher. No one shall share this title, or part of this title, to any social media or file hosting websites.

The moral right of Lee Coffey to be identified as author of this work has been asserted in accordance with Section 77 of the Copyright, Designs and Patents Act 1988.

USE OF COPYRIGHTED MUSIC

A licence issued by Concord Theatricals to perform this play does not include permission to use the incidental music specified in this publication. In the United Kingdom: Where the place of performance is already licensed by the PERFORMING RIGHT SOCIETY (PRS) a return of the music used must be made to them. If the place of performance is not so licensed then application should be made to PRS for Music (www.prsformusic.com). A separate and additional licence from PHONOGRAPHIC PERFORMANCE LTD (www.ppluk.com) may be needed whenever commercial recordings are used. Outside the United Kingdom: Please contact the appropriate music licensing authority in your territory for the rights to any incidental music.

USE OF COPYRIGHTED THIRD-PARTY MATERIALS

Licensees are solely responsible for obtaining formal written permission from copyright owners to use copyrighted third-party materials (e.g., artworks, logos) in the performance of this play and are strongly cautioned to do so. If no such permission is obtained by the licensee, then the licensee must use only original materials that the licensee owns and controls. Licensees are solely responsible and liable for clearances of all third-party copyrighted materials, and shall indemnify the copyright owners of the play(s) and their licensing agent, Concord Theatricals Ltd., against any costs, expenses, losses and liabilities arising from the use of such copyrighted third-party materials by licensees.

IMPORTANT BILLING AND CREDIT REQUIREMENTS

If you have obtained performance rights to this title, please refer to your licensing agreement for important billing and credit requirements.

G.O.D. (GOOD. ORDERLY. DIRECTION.) opened in Axis Ballymun on 4th October 2022 as a part of The Dublin Theatre Festival. Produced by Bitter Like A Lemon in association with Axis, Ballymun. Supported by Irish Theatre Institute, The Arts Council of Ireland, The Rutland Centre and Dublin Port Company. The cast were as follows:

KATE	Lauren Larkin
STEPHEN	Luke Griffin
DAVE	Loré Adewusi
REBECCA	Andrea Irvine
DAMIEN	Simon O'Gorman
CHRISTINE	Amilia Stewart Keating

CREATIVES:

Director	Eoghan Carrick
Writer	Lee Coffey
Lighting Designer	Eoin Winning
Set and Costume Designer	Ellen Kirk
Sound Design	Sinead Diskin
Stage Manager	Eoin Harrington
Fight Director	Ciaran O'Grady
Production Manager	Shane Morgan
Promotional Design	Sadhbh McLoughlin

Bitter Like a Lemon

Bitter Like a Lemon is a new writing company giving a platform to working-class voices of Dublin, consisting of Actor/Producer/Director Amilia Stewart, Producer/Stage Manager Evie McGuinness and Playwright Lee Coffey.

Their first production *Leper + Chip*, by Lee Coffey and directed Karl Shiels premiered in Theatre Upstairs in 2014 and toured Ireland and internationally. *A Boy called Nedd* by Emily Gilmor-Murphy, directed by Karl Shiels and *Peruvian Voodoo*, written and directed by Lee Coffey were produced alongside each other in 2015. In 2016 they produced Lee Coffey's third play *Slice, the Thief*, directed by Jeda De Bri. In 2017 they were the company in residence in Axis Ballymun, developing their next show *From All Sides*, which premiered in Dublin Fringe Festival 2017, co-produced with Axis Ballymun. During this residency they also produced a work in progress showing of *Nothin' But A Toerag* by Aisling O'Mara. *Murder of Crows* by Lee Coffey, directed by Karl Shiels premiered in Theatre Upstairs in 2016 and toured Ireland in 2018. In 2018, Bitter Like a Lemon were commissioned by Dublin Port Company to develop a play about the history of Dublin's dock workers as a part of their Port Perspectives initiative. In 2019, *In Our Veins* by Lee Coffey, premiered as a part of The Abbey Theatre's 2019 season. *G.O.D (Good. Orderly. Direction.)* which will premiere in as a part of Dublin Theatre Festival 2022.

CHARACTERS

KATE – late 20s
STEPHEN – early 50s
DAVE – early 20s
REBECCA – mid 50s
DAMIEN – mid 50s
CHRISTINE – mid 30s

SETTING

The Lakelands Centre, Dublin.

TIME

Over the course of a year.

AUTHOR'S NOTES

G.O.D. (Good. Orderly. Direction.) is a play about human beings and their stories. We know very little about recovery as a society but we know a lot about addiction. People think you're sober and then that's it. That's what I thought when I started the journey in writing this play. We've seen and spoken about addiction – active addiction – but what about active recovery? When somebody has come through rehab, they're sober but need the tools to live their lives normally. That's when recovery comes in and these people dedicate two years – minimum – of their lives to getting better. To coming to terms with what they've done, who they've hurt and who they once were.

This play tells those stories and doesn't hide behind the reality of what faces aftercare users on a daily basis. The struggles, the losses and the victories.

This play is for those that fight that fight. Those that show up, one day at a time and keep coming back.

THANK YOU

Carla Kelly, Miriam and Vincent Boyle, Mark Whelan, Ray Smith, Mark O'Brien, Niamh Ní Chonchubhair, Dublin Port Company, Denis Coffey, Catherine Coffey, The team at Irish Theatre Institute, Ger Kellett, Liam Carney, Stephen Jones, Una Kavanagh, Hilda Fay, John Cronin, Derek Magee, Conall Keating, The Rutland Centre and to all those that opened up and trusted me with their stories.

For those that keep coming back.

Scene One

(The play takes place over the course of a year. It is set in an aftercare recovery group in The Lakelands Centre, Dublin, Ireland. Scenes jump time, never place.)

(Lights up. 13th January. A small room in The Lakelands Centre, Dublin. **STEPHEN** *is setting up chairs. He stands in the room for a few moments, looks around. He takes a breath. Pause.)*

(Lights down.)

Scene Two

(Lights up. 13th January. From here on, all scenes drop into moments, not seeing what has gone before or after, just moments of a two hour long session. A meeting room in The Lakelands Centre, Dublin. Aftercare group members – **DAMIEN, DAVE, REBECCA, CHRISTINE, KATE** *and their facilitator,* **STEPHEN.***)*

STEPHEN. Thanks, everyone. So Kate, first day so you just sit and listen. I'll check in with you later.

KATE. Okay.

STEPHEN. So everyone, em, not sure how to say this but I've a bit of housekeeping. Michael's relapsed and he's gone back out.

DAVE. What?

STEPHEN. We've lost contact with him.

(Pause.)

DAVE. No…

REBECCA. What a shame.

CHRISTINE. Poor Michael.

(The group process the news. **DAMIEN** *makes eye contact with* **STEPHEN.** *Pause.)*

STEPHEN. How are you feeling, Damien?

(Pause.)

DAMIEN. I'm okay.

STEPHEN. You're okay?

DAMIEN. It's never nice when someone goes back out but... I don't know, I guess... I wasn't as close to him.

STEPHEN. Do you not relate to Michael?

DAMIEN. Course, I do.

STEPHEN. More than most here, I'd say.

DAMIEN. Yeah. I've been him. I've relapsed. Given in to those voices after two years of aftercare.

STEPHEN. And you say you've been okay?

DAMIEN. I suppose I understand where he's at right now. Something obviously triggered him and he succumbed to it.

STEPHEN. Does that not remind you of your own relapse?

DAMIEN. Yeah, it does.

STEPHEN. And you're okay with that?

DAMIEN. I've started to think about why? Why we're like this. Why we're always looking for that escape.

STEPHEN. There isn't just one reason.

DAMIEN. I know that, we all have our reasons. But by trying to block it out before that might have been the reason I fell last time. So I'm trying to think about it more. And that's okay, because that's how I can move on. Michael's relapse will add to that, it shows how precarious this all is. Which is good/

(Pause.)

DAVE. I don't think it's good that Michael went back out.

DAMIEN. That's not what I was saying.

DAVE. Sounds like you were.

DAMIEN. I was saying it was good because it brings to light my own struggles. Which is good, no?

STEPHEN. It is, Damien.

DAVE. It's not good. Michael is gone. He was one of the strongest in this group.

CHRISTINE. Clearly wasn't.

DAVE. Excuse me? He was stronger than you anyway.

CHRISTINE. Still here, am I not?

STEPHEN. Come on, let's not.

(Pause.)

Go on, Dave.

DAVE. I'm not okay with this. This… this is bad.

STEPHEN. It's okay, let's think of the positive. You had a really great breakthrough last week.

DAVE. I did and now this comes along. When does it stop, you know? I was close to Michael, he was my friend. Rebecca was too and/

REBECCA. It's okay, Dave. He'd want us to let it all out.

DAVE. How are you with all this, Rebecca?

REBECCA. Not good.

STEPHEN. Everything's okay, you're both here and we can work through this.

DAMIEN. That's true, youngfella.

(Pause.)

DAVE. I'm worried. This week wasn't a good week and now, now this!

STEPHEN. It was a bad week, Dave. They're going to happen but you're here and you didn't break.

(Pause.)

CHRISTINE. Did you not?

> *(Pause.)*

DAVE. Eh... Tuesday night. Sarah was asleep and I went for a walk.

> *(Pause.)*

Around the block and at the end of the road, there's this shop. Off-licence. The light flashing on and off. It was like it was calling me, you know?

CHRISTINE. Know too well.

DAVE. I stood there. Must have been an hour, maybe two. Knowing full well, if I went in there, one sup and I'd be gone. Back to where I was.

> *(Slight pause.)*

STEPHEN. What did you do, Dave?

DAVE. The flash of the light. Like it was just banging and banging, piercing the side of my skull.

STEPHEN. What did you do, Dave?

DAVE. I ran. Home, and when I say I ran. I fucking ran, bolted it, like my lungs were going to burst. Till I made it home. Slammed the door, fell to the floor... and I bawled my eyes out.

> *(Pause. A silence falls on the group. Every one of them has been in **DAVE**'s position.)*

Sarah came running down the stairs. I told her what happened and she... just held me.

> *(Pause.)*

STEPHEN. How did that make you feel, Dave?

DAVE. Hopeless. Is this what our lives are to be?

> *(Lights down.)*

Scene Three

(Lights up. 27th January. The Lakelands Centre, Dublin. The same set up as before, maybe people are in different seats.)

REBECCA. It was an interesting week.

STEPHEN. How so?

REBECCA. I was thinking of Damien.

DAMIEN. Thinking of me will only get you in trouble, Missus.

(He ends with a smile.)

REBECCA. *(Playfully.)* Don't flatter yourself. I was thinking of Dave too.

DAVE. I'm very happy with Sarah but appreciate the gesture.

REBECCA. It's always sex with men, isn't it?

CHRISTINE. With Damien it is anyway.

*(**DAMIEN** laughs.)*

STEPHEN. Now, now.

CHRISTINE. I was only messing, Damien.

DAMIEN. I know, love.

STEPHEN. Go on, Rebecca.

REBECCA. Well, I was thinking of them both. Dave's comment a few weeks ago, how he ran. Ran from the off-licence, home to Sarah. And I was thinking of Damien's relapse. The difference between them. We all have something to run from, otherwise we wouldn't be here. But maybe, we all don't have something to run to. Something good to run to. A friend, a family member… a Sarah. *(Pause.)* Am I making sense?

DAMIEN. So you're saying I don't have anything in my life?

REBECCA. I didn't mean it like that.

CHRISTINE. Sounded like it.

REBECCA. What I'm saying is we are all running. We all need to find something safe to run to. To help. When the darkest thoughts come for us.

DAVE. If I didn't have Sarah, I know where I would have run to.

REBECCA. Exactly. Damien, you haven't got that Sarah and neither have I.

DAMIEN. I can't be with anyone right now.

REBECCA. I don't mean that we all need somebody. We all need a Sarah, which can be anything, I suppose, that helps us with those dark thoughts. Am I going mad?

STEPHEN. You're not.

DAVE. You're making sense, Rebecca.

KATE. Yeah.

CHRISTINE. She speaks/

STEPHEN. Christine, please.

REBECCA. Well, as a child, I used to swim a lot. My father would bring us. I remember feeling free in the water, that I hadn't a care in the world. So this week, I went down to the forty foot and I jumped in.

DAMIEN. You mad bitch.

CHRISTINE. It's Baltic.

REBECCA. Thought I was going to have a heart attack.

STEPHEN. Did it help you?

REBECCA. It did. It felt the exact same as it did, all those years ago. I felt free, light, completely weightless.

DAMIEN. Not a hope.

REBECCA. It made me happy, made me smile.

(Pause.)

STEPHEN. Maybe that's your Sarah.

DAMIEN. Well, if you're right. I hope my Sarah is something above freezing.

(Pause.)

STEPHEN. Glad you're starting to explore and implement ways to help yourself, Rebecca.

REBECCA. It may not apply to everyone. It could be a load of bollocks or it could be a step in the right direction. Something good to run to. A Sarah.

DAVE. *(Smiling.)* Is that what it's being christened?

DAMIEN. I think it works.

(Pause.)

CHRISTINE. What if you've already lost your Sarah?

(Pause. Lights down.)

Scene Four

(Lights up. 10th February. The Lakelands Centre, Dublin. The same set up as before, maybe people are in different seats.)

DAMIEN. My week was grand enough, yeah. I was up in my sister's and the nephew has been getting into trouble in school. He's fourteen, of course he's getting into trouble. Who didn't?

DAVE. Have to say, I was a little bastard in school.

CHRISTINE. I didn't really have any interest.

DAMIEN. Not many of us do. Those that did, they're doctors now or whatever/

DAVE. And look at us.

DAMIEN. A bunch of basket cases.

CHRISTINE. Speak for yourself.

DAMIEN. I am speaking for you, love.

CHRISTINE. Whatever.

(Pause.)

DAMIEN. So he was expelled. I thought my sister was going to murder him.

DAVE. What he do?

DAMIEN. He threw a book at his teacher.

CHRISTINE. Jaysus.

DAMIEN. Yeah and he sent him to the principal's office.

DAVE. Standard.

DAMIEN. Now, this teacher wears a wig. A bad one. You know those ones? Look like there's a dead animal just lying there.

DAVE. They freak me out. Like, why?

DAMIEN. I know.

DAVE. Just go baldy gracefully, man.

DAMIEN. Well, as he was leaving. He grabbed the wig off his head, popped it on and jumped out the window.

CHRISTINE. Piss off, he didn't.

DAMIEN. He's a mad little bastard. Out the window, onto the shed and stuck it to the window of the class next door.

CHRISTINE. Imaginative.

DAMIEN. Funny.

DAVE. Cruel.

CHRISTINE. Yeah.

DAMIEN. But funny.

DAVE. Gas.

CHRISTINE. Very funny.

STEPHEN. Are we done?

>   *(Pause. **DAMIEN** notices that **STEPHEN** is just staring at him.)*

DAMIEN. Done with what?

STEPHEN. What are we doing here?

DAMIEN. Talking.

STEPHEN. What are you all doing here?

DAMIEN. We're just talking, Stephen. Like we always do.

STEPHEN. You're rambling.

DAVE. Just listening to Damien's story about his week/

STEPHEN. We are not here to tell pointless stories. Used to deflect away from why you're all here. You are here to talk. Not about that, about yourself.

DAMIEN. It was just a story/

STEPHEN. Exactly, come on. Why would we waste time? Your time, my time. On Damien's nephew. As funny or as mental as that child may be, it's not helpful to us. Do you think it's helpful, Christine?

CHRISTINE. No… but it was funny/

STEPHEN. You all don't want to talk about yourselves, get to the root of why you're here?

DAVE. We do.

STEPHEN. Well stupid, pointless stories won't get us there!

(Lights down.)

Scene Five

(Lights up. Scene five. 17th March. The Lakelands Centre, Dublin. After a session. **STEPHEN** *and* **KATE**.*)*

STEPHEN. Are you able for this, Kate?

(We focus on her for a moment and the light flashes out.)

Scene Six

(Lights up. 24th March. The Lakelands Centre, Dublin. The same set up as before, maybe people are in different seats.)

DAMIEN. It's funny. What Rebecca said a few weeks ago. About me having nothing to run to. No Sarah, no G.O.D. She was right. That night that I relapsed, I went looking for sex. Went straight back to the old haunts.

(Pause.)

STEPHEN. Why do you think you went?

DAMIEN. I don't know.

STEPHEN. Come on, Damien. I know you well enough to know/

DAMIEN. I don't know. I was feeling the urge, I needed that escape.

STEPHEN. What happened that day? That made you need to escape.

DAMIEN. That's the worrying thing, I don't know.

(Pause.)

STEPHEN. Okay, fair enough. Just relax for a bit. We'll come back to you.

DAVE. I've been there, Damien.

REBECCA. Me too.

STEPHEN. You're not the only one, Damien. Kate, have you ever felt like that?

KATE. Yes.

STEPHEN. And did you know what you wanted to escape from?

KATE. Yes.

STEPHEN. Go on ahead.

(Pause. **KATE** *thinks for a moment.)*

KATE. Could we come back to me?

STEPHEN. Okay, you talk when you're ready. Christine, what about you?

CHRISTINE. I've always known why.

(Pause.)

It's always just her. I do be fine, walking down the street or I'm at the shops. Then I see something. Something she liked, or I see her face in another little girl's.

(Pause.)

I just see her smile. Everywhere.

(Pause.)

That image, is burnt into my brain and I can't get it out... and I don't want to. But at the same time, when I see it, it hurts me. Right down... right down to my soul, you know?

(Pause.)

STEPHEN. Losing a child is/

CHRISTINE. I didn't lose her, she was taken from me.

(Pause.)

I miss her. It gets unbearable at times and that's when I want to just... forget.

(Pause.)

STEPHEN. Twelve months sober, Christine.

DAVE. One day at a time.

KATE. I hope I can get to twelve months.

STEPHEN. You will.

DAVE. One day at a time.

CHRISTINE. Why are we going on like it's that easy?

STEPHEN. We're not.

REBECCA. We all know it's not, Christine. It's not easy. You just need to find something that calms you down. Helps you.

CHRISTINE. It's great that you have something, Rebecca. It really is. But one day at a time, can feel like a year!

DAMIEN. Come on, Christine. Don't/

CHRISTINE. You know more than anyone.

DAMIEN. We all know/

CHRISTINE. You're back. You left, you were gone and now you're back!

DAMIEN. I'm well aware.

CHRISTINE. And what caused that? Go on, say it. "I don't know!" You do know! We always know what makes us want to escape. One day at a time! One day at a time! One day at a fucking time!

(Lights down.)

Scene Seven

(Lights up. 14th April. The Lakelands Centre, Dublin. The same set up as before, maybe people are in different seats.)

DAVE. One day at a time. As we always say. Myself and Sarah have just been getting on so well. Better than ever, you know?

(Pause.)

You know what she did the other day?

(Pause.)

She looked at me and she said, "I'm really proud of you, Dave."

(Pause.)

You know when your missus says something, and it's not like her. Right, so without Sarah, I'd be lost, right? But, but when she said it, I was thinking, "What are you up to? What's your angle here, love?" You know what I mean?

(Pause.)

I was sceptical.

STEPHEN. You don't think she meant it?

DAVE. She's never been proud of me before, or didn't say it anyway. So with everything going so well it threw me, you know? Like, how can she be proud of me? All the shit I did. Being out of it nonstop. Avoiding her, robbing her/lying to her/

STEPHEN. Robbing her?

*(**DAVE** realises that he's never mentioned that in class before.)*

DAVE. Yeah. I... I robbed her. I robbed Sarah.

> *(Pause.)*

It was a couple of months before I went to rehab.

> *(Pause.)*

STEPHEN. What did you rob, Dave?

DAVE. There was a little girl from the estate. Casey was her name. She had this rare form of cancer. Everyone was doing bits, you know? Fundraisers. This and that. Sarah did one. It was... a sponsored walk round the area.

> *(Pause. You can see that* **DAVE** *is reluctant but keeps going nonetheless.)*

She raised five hundred quid. Left it upstairs in the dresser. And I... I took it.

> *(Pause. Nobody speaks. It just sits on the room for a moment.)*

A child with cancer and I took her money to get high.

> *(****DAVE*** *sits for a moment, thinking about it. Nobody speaks.)*

She never even suspected me. I was hiding it so well, you know? Still working, holding it all together. I said we were broken into. And that the back window was open.

> *(Pause.)*

Little Casey died a few months ago. And... it still eats me up, man, you know? Just digging away at me. I couldn't believe Sarah never left me when I told her the truth. She forgave me.

> *(Pause.)*

When she said it, I guess I just thought... how could you be proud of a scumbag like me?

(Pause.)

I just didn't think I deserved it. That praise.

(Pause.)

STEPHEN. You do, Dave. You had the strength to tell her. To tell us. That's a huge step.

(Pause.)

DAVE. Yeah, I suppose.

STEPHEN. It's out there now and look, feel it, and use that as motivation. To never get to that point again.

DAVE. Yeah, man. For Sarah.

STEPHEN. And for little Casey too.

(Pause.)

DAVE. Want to hear something funny?

STEPHEN. Always.

DAVE. The day she died, I went to her house. Put five hundred in an envelope and dropped it in the letter box. *(Pause.)* As if that would change anything.

*(A longer pause than those gone before. They let **DAVE** sit in his thoughts.)*

STEPHEN. I'll come back to you in a while, Dave. See how you are.

(Pause.)

REBECCA. I can completely relate to that, Dave. When we have a good day, a good week. We feel like we don't deserve it and it brings us back to that... shame, the guilt of what has gone before. Joy brings us to sorrow but we can have good days and I've realised that that's okay to say. I was almost afraid to say that before, in case I'd jinx myself. You feel unworthy of it and I do... or did. All the time.

(Pause.)

Remember I told you that I started swimming? I went again this week, first thing before work. The water is warming up, bleedin' slowly but it's getting there. I don't give a shite anymore, I just jump in.

(Pause.)

All the anxiety just seems to melt away. I go most mornings now and it really screws the head on. There's been this woman the past few mornings. Looking at me. Not in a way that worried me or anything. Just giving me the eyes. You know those eyes?

KATE. Like she was going to batter you?

REBECCA. *(Laughing.)* No.

KATE. They're the eyes I've been given.

REBECCA. Well, I swim like I'm about to drown so I thought it could have been concern.

KATE. Thought you said you could swim?

REBECCA. I can, I just swim a little wonky.

KATE. Wonky.

REBECCA. Yes.

KATE. Right.

REBECCA. But I can move. This was going on all week. I'd be getting in. She'd be looking at me. I'd be getting out. She'd be looking at me. In the water. She'd be looking at me. Always looking at me. It was relentless but then this morning. She walks over to me.

KATE. Not swim over to you?

REBECCA. *(Laughing.)* No, we had gotten out/

KATE. Ah right.

REBECCA. She walked over.

KATE. Like she was going to batter you?

REBECCA. No, I told you. Not those kind of eyes.

KATE. Sure?

REBECCA. Yes.

KATE. Sounds it.

STEPHEN. Kate.

KATE. What?

STEPHEN. It's great that you're getting involved but there's a time to join the conversation and a time to listen. You're just cutting in a little too much.

KATE. Oh, sorry.

STEPHEN. What's everyone else doing?

> *(Pause.* **KATE** *looks at everyone else – realising that they're listening – and sits back in her chair.)*

Go ahead, Rebecca.

REBECCA. She said, "Is your name Rebecca?" I told her that it was. She said, "I've been looking at you the past few weeks." When I was talking to her, she was so familiar and I couldn't place why. Then she asks me if my mother's name was Annie. I told her it was. Well, didn't she jump on me/

KATE. Told ya'!

STEPHEN. I mean it, Kate. I'll throw you out/

REBECCA. Hugging me and hugging me! She was so happy and she was cheering. I was a little freaked out but didn't she tell me who she was and... I couldn't believe it.

KATE. Well?

STEPHEN. Kate/

REBECCA. My cousin, Maggie.

KATE. Anti-climax.

STEPHEN. Right, get out, you!

(STEPHEN stands up and pushes KATE towards the door.)

KATE. You can't do that.

REBECCA. He can.

STEPHEN. I can.

KATE. I'm sorry.

STEPHEN. I'll see you next week. Seeing as though you've found your voice, you can start the session next week.

(KATE exits. STEPHEN sits.)

She has to learn. So, your cousin.

REBECCA. Can you believe it? We hadn't seen each other in years. Families drift apart and ours did. It was like the universe was putting something good in my way. Helping me again. She was so lovely. Jesus, it was about twenty years since I'd last seen her. How mad is that? I just happen to start swimming in that exact place. She lives out there, we're meeting tomorrow morning. Going for a swim and having breakfast. Tomorrow. I couldn't help but smile.

(Lights down.)

Scene Eight

(Lights up. 21st April. The Lakelands Centre, Dublin. The same set up as before, maybe people are in different seats. **KATE** *is hyperventilating. The others watch on.)*

STEPHEN. Are you okay, Kate? We're all here for you.

*(***KATE*** calms down slightly.)*

It's okay, Kate. But eventually. You will have to talk.

(Lights down.)

Scene Nine

(Lights up. 5th May. The Lakelands Centre, Dublin. The same set up as before, maybe people are in different seats.)

CHRISTINE. I don't want to.

STEPHEN. It's something you need to talk about.

CHRISTINE. It's not that easy.

STEPHEN. We know it's not easy but you need to talk.

CHRISTINE. Talk, you say that all the time. Do you know how hard that is?

STEPHEN. I do but to move on and get better, we have to.

CHRISTINE. We have to. We. WE! There is no we, it's you and us.

DAMIEN. Come on, will you?

STEPHEN. Christine, I'm here to help you. To listen and to help.

CHRISTINE. You're here to judge.

STEPHEN. I don't judge anyone in here.

CHRISTINE. Me bollocks/

DAVE. Would you stop/

STEPHEN. Christine/

CHRISTINE. Sitting there and thanking your lucky stars that you're not one of us/

STEPHEN. Is that so/

CHRISTINE. Addicts/

REBECCA. Christine/

CHRISTINE. It's hard/

DAVE. Desperately floating above the surf, praying we don't sink.

STEPHEN. Dave, one moment, okay?

DAVE. Sorry.

(STEPHEN takes a second.)

STEPHEN. I know what it's like to sink/

CHRISTINE. Sink into your chair, yeah.

STEPHEN. Ever think how I got here?

(Pause.)

I sat exactly where you are today.

CHRISTINE. What?

(Pause.)

STEPHEN. I came through rehab, came through aftercare, just as you are. Just as you all are. I sat there and I spoke about what I'd done, who I'd hurt, how the heroin just took me. Every part of me. I was at its mercy.

(Pause.)

CHRISTINE. Heroin?

STEPHEN. Heroin. Sober fourteen years. So when I tell you all that I understand what you're going through. I understand *exactly* what you're going through.

(Pause.)

CHRISTINE. I didn't know.

STEPHEN. How would you? It's not usually something we get into but yes, I was in active addiction for six years. I hurt a lot of people. Lost my family, lost my friends and I hit the very bottom.

DAVE. Man, that's deadly.

REBECCA. What?

DAVE. Not the losing your family and friends part. The fact that you were here, and came through it all. You're one of us.

STEPHEN. One and the same.

DAVE. That's deadly, isn't it, Damien?

> (**DAMIEN** *says nothing.*)

Damien?

DAMIEN. It is, yeah.

STEPHEN. Damien already knew.

CHRISTINE. You knew/

DAVE. And you never told us?

DAMIEN. It's Stephen's to tell.

DAVE. You sly bastard, ya'!

STEPHEN. He's right. It's my story to tell. Just as your story is yours to tell. So how about some of you tell it?

> (*There is a universal feeling of hope throughout the group. Conveyed with smiles from some and nothing from others.*)

DAVE. Here, I don't give a bollocks. Everyone up.

REBECCA. What?

DAVE. Everyone up. Come on.

> (*Everyone stands up except* **DAMIEN**.)

Come on, even you, you old bastard.

> (**DAMIEN** *stands.*)

DAMIEN. You little shite.

DAVE. Right, Stephen. I just want to say. You're a fucking inspiration, man.

> *(He starts to clap his hands, slowly joined by everyone.)*

If you can do it. We can all fucking do it!

> *(The cheering continues. Lights down.)*

Scene Ten

(Lights up. 19th May. The Lakelands Centre, Dublin. **STEPHEN** *sits alone. He looks at his phone, sighs and stares into nothing. He sits alone for a moment. Until he's taken out of it by the entering group. Lights down.)*

Scene Eleven

(Lights up. 2nd June. The Lakelands Centre, Dublin. The same set up as before, maybe people are in different seats. **KATE** *is filled with nervous energy, it's her first time opening up. She speaks quickly.)*

KATE. The drink was a way for me to forget it all.

(Slight pause.)

Everything. I, eh, only ever really had my nan.

(Slight pause.)

She loved me and I loved her. She passed away when I was eight and that was it, I suppose. The last time I felt love.

(Slight pause.)

I mean, I had family but they were never really there, you know? My parents didn't like to show emotion.

(Slight pause.)

What little girl doesn't want a hug from their ma? So, I grew up without that... warmth, you know? That love that most of the children in my class got. They settled in with each other, made friends, were as I hadn't a clue. Didn't know how to act, I didn't know how to just be a kid. Became that outsider that every class has.

(Slight pause.)

I kept to myself, and eventually made a few friends. We started to hang out after school. It was nice and one day, Carol Cleary got us a bottle of wine. We were sixteen and that's what all the girls were doing. We went to the canal and three of us drank it.

(Slight pause.)

STEPHEN. Was that your first time drinking?

KATE. Yeah. I felt on top of the world. It grabbed me and didn't let go. We started to do it most days. Try our best to get some drink. From anywhere. A few weeks ago, you were all talking about it and I didn't say anything but I knew exactly what you meant. That escape. That high of... just feeling good for once. Like someone else. Like someone new.

(Slight pause. They all sit and think of that moment. A mutual bond they have.)

Then once you become eighteen, it all just gets so much easier, doesn't it? No more hiding or thinking of who could buy us drink. We could. And we did. I got into college and everything so it was just parties. Freshers' week, rag week, and that's the college life. You never think you've a problem because, well, everyone is doing it.

(Pause.)

Then I dropped out. Fell behind. Failed a few exams. Needed to repeat a few at the end of the year, em, five, I think.

(Pause.)

I was going in locked. Thinking nobody noticed but *everyone* noticed. Miles behind and you also had to pay to repeat the exams and I'd no money. And any I had, it wasn't going towards exams.

(Pause.)

I was working part time in a bar, which wasn't helping anything. I picked up more shifts. And that place was worse than college. Drinks after every single shift.

(Pause.)

I was living at home. My parents split, my da moved... somewhere. So it was me and my ma. She'd be working all day, I'd be working all night. Ships in the night. That just kept on going and now... here I am.

(Slightly longer pause.)

STEPHEN. Are you okay?

KATE. Yeah.

STEPHEN. That's a good start, Kate.

(Pause.)

How are you feeling?

KATE. Shite.

STEPHEN. Shite is not a feeling. How are you feeling?

KATE. Em... sad, I suppose.

STEPHEN. You suppose?

KATE. I'm sad.

STEPHEN. Okay. You need to connect with what you're feeling and allow yourself to feel it. Okay? That's only natural after opening up for the first time.

DAMIEN. Gets easier, kid.

STEPHEN. It does.

REBECCA. We've all been there.

STEPHEN. Look, you spoke about it and you're still alive. We just need to talk and know that everything will be okay.

KATE. Yeah, it's okay.

STEPHEN. There you go. It's okay.

KATE. It's okay.

STEPHEN. Say it again.

KATE. It's okay.

STEPHEN. What is it?

KATE. IT'S OKAY!

> *(Lights down.)*

Scene Twelve

(Lights up. 16th June. The Lakelands Centre, Dublin. The same set up as before, maybe people are in different seats.)

DAVE. Right, everyone. I've news.

(Pause.)

I'm going to be a dad.

(Some stand and cheer.)

I know, I can't believe it. Me, a dad?

REBECCA. You'll be an amazing father.

KATE. So happy for you.

DAMIEN. Great news, kid.

DAVE. I didn't even know it worked.

DAMIEN. Alright, let's not go into detail.

DAVE. Afraid you'll like it?

CHRISTINE. I'm so happy for you, Dave.

(Pause.)

DAVE. Oh, Christine. I'm so sorry.

CHRISTINE. Would you stop/

DAVE. No, here I am, bleeding, boasting/

CHRISTINE. Dave/

DAVE. I'm a dope.

CHRISTINE. Dave/

DAVE. Yeah?

CHRISTINE. Don't be stupid. I'm delighted for you. You deserve something good in your life.

DAVE. I just couldn't wait to tell you all.

> *(Pause.)*

Sometimes, our interactions seem to be all negative so it was nice to have something positive to say.

> *(Pause.* **DAVE** *sits, thinking, with a smile on his face. Everyone watches him and lets him have his moment.)*

STEPHEN. It is nice to have something positive to say. You're going to be a brilliant father.

DAVE. Hopefully, yeah. As happy as I am. Those doubts just pop in there, don't they?

DAMIEN. We all have those doubts, Dave.

DAVE. It's one thing being an addict and destroying your own life but a little child's, you know?

DAMIEN. All this will give you is more motivation.

DAVE. That's what you'd hope, isn't it? Sarah and the baby.

DAMIEN. Exactly.

STEPHEN. We've started on a high today, haven't we?

REBECCA. Straight out of the traps.

STEPHEN. Care to follow that, Rebecca?

REBECCA. I don't know, it's a tough act to follow.

DAVE. I always am.

REBECCA. *(Smiling.)* Don't I know it.

> *(Pause.)*

Well to tie in with what Dave is saying and the conversation around families growing. I've been spending a lot of time with my Cousin Maggie.

STEPHEN. That really was a special thing to happen.

REBECCA. I know and when I needed it too. Someone might be looking out for me, you never know. We met a couple of times this week and went for lunch out in Bray on Sunday.

KATE. I was in Bray on Sunday too. Sorry, don't throw me out again.

STEPHEN. I won't be throwing you out.

KATE. Felt like a moment I could join in.

(**STEPHEN** *smiles.*)

STEPHEN. I'll give you the benefit of the doubt.

KATE. Sorry, Rebecca.

REBECCA. You're grand, love. Would have been nice to see you.

(**KATE** *smiles.*)

We headed down and walked on the pier. Maggie had brought her daughter, Aine and her little granddaughter, Susie. Gorgeous little thing she is. So more family members that I never knew I even had. Our families are growing, Dave.

(**DAVE** *smiles.*)

The day was… it was really nice. We spent the whole day, just walking around, we had a little picnic and that. Near the end of the day, we were outside the amusements. Maggie and Aine were messing with the pram, trying to get it ready or something. Didn't the little one leg it off. Straight into the casino.

(*Pause.*)

Without even thinking, I ran after her. If I'd seen where she ran to, maybe I wouldn't have but, yeah, I did.

(*Pause.*)

I looked up, saw where I was and, and it all came rushing back to me. The lights, the music, the sound of the coins hitting the back of the machine. The familiar. The soundtrack to my escape. You see, Kate/

KATE. Me?

REBECCA. Yes, I want to tell you this. I was never into horse racing or poker or drink or anything like that. For me, it was the slot machines

KATE. The ones with the big handle?

REBECCA. One in the same. They were my vice. I'd sit in front of them for hours, for the whole day.

KATE. Not get bored, no?

REBECCA. I couldn't. They just kept me there. You'd lose, play again. Lose, play again. You'd win, get the rush and play again.

KATE. How did you get lost in them?

REBECCA. A bit like yourself, my parents never had time for me, no affection. They drank and wouldn't be present at all. But one year my parents brought me on holidays. They drank and I wandered around the amusements, eventually finding a slot machine. When I pulled that lever, it was over for me, I was gone, free and I felt like I was floating on air. Weightless. I know that you feel that too.

KATE. I do.

REBECCA. Everyone here has, the means are just different.

KATE. Drink.

DAVE. Drink and drugs.

DAMIEN. Sex.

CHRISTINE. Drink.

REBECCA. Gambling. I'd spend all day at those slots. I'd run out of money and then try get some more, so I could go back. It's like there was this, elastic, attached to me, pulling me back. No matter how far I ran, I would be pulled straight back. When I grew up, I started to work. I'd spend my whole week's wages on the slots. Leaving, absolutely broke after a couple of hours. I'd cry to my mother, saying I'm sorry and that it wouldn't happen again.

(Pause.)

KATE. But it did/

REBECCA. It always did.

KATE. I always felt so powerless.

REBECCA. Me too. So for me to be standing in this place, with all that coming back to me/

KATE. Wasn't good/

REBECCA. Not in the slightest. I hadn't been in a casino since before I started rehab.

*(**REBECCA** takes a long pause. **STEPHEN** is visibly worried and cuts in.)*

STEPHEN. What happened, Rebecca?

(Pause.)

REBECCA. I looked down at the little one. The slots sounding in the background. Sounding and sounding. Piercing my brain, calling me, screaming at me. Then she looked up at me and smiled.

(Pause.)

I smiled back, picked her up and I walked out.

(Pause. A smile crosses her face.)

STEPHEN. How did you feel?

REBECCA. After it, I gave her to Aine and I went to the toilet. I walked in, closed the door and I… I cried my eyes out. Not because I was sad, I just didn't really know what to be feeling, you know? I felt terrified, and calm, all at the same time. I stood looking at myself in the mirror. For what felt like days. And that's all I did. Just stared at myself.

> *(Slight pause.)*

Then I took a minute, headed back to my family and we went about our day.

> *(Slight pause.)*

The best thing was, I had no urge to walk back into that casino. None at all. I felt normal. For the first time… in a very… long time.

> *(Slight pause. **STEPHEN** knows that she's gotten through a lot today. He moves the session on.)*

STEPHEN. Have to say, very proud of you, Rebecca.

DAMIEN. Making us all look bad.

CHRISTINE. A day of good news. You and this fella.

DAVE. That's one big victory, Rebecca.

REBECCA. Yeah, I guess it is. I think it was the little one, Susie, that got me through.

DAVE. Children, a God send.

> *(**CHRISTINE** drops her head.)*

REBECCA. You'll have a little helper of your own soon.

DAVE. I will.

REBECCA. You will.

DAMIEN. Too right, you will. Dibs on Godfather.

(They all laugh.)

Me fucking arse!

(Lights down.)

Scene Thirteen

(Lights up. 30th June. The Lakelands Centre, Dublin. The same set up as before, maybe people are in different seats.)

STEPHEN. Are you being completely honest with yourself?

KATE. I am.

STEPHEN. Your rock bottom was you, stumbling out of a pub.

KATE. Yeah.

STEPHEN. People stumble out of pubs on a weekly basis, Kate.

KATE. So?

STEPHEN. So, I just find it a little hard to believe.

KATE. That's what it was. I fell out, on to the ground and I knew something had to change.

STEPHEN. Okay.

KATE. So I/

STEPHEN. One second, Kate.

(Pause. Each person tells the story of their breaking point.)

You've all spoken about it. Your rock bottom. Mine, was when I woke up in my daughter Michaela's room with a needle in my arm. I broke in. My ex-wife screaming, my daughter crying, me lying on the floor.

(Pause. There is nothing said or laid out, everyone just organically joins the conversation.)

REBECCA. My mother had dementia. So I'd pick up her pension. Every week. Then I'd lose it on the slots. Every week. Then one day I took it and went on a binge, I must have been in that casino for... couldn't even tell you. But I didn't check on her in that time and... she'd died. Lying there alone while I gambled away her money.

(Pause.)

DAMIEN. I was caught in bed with our neighbour. My ex-wife walked in on the two of us. Me, him, in our bed. Thought trying it with a man could give me a bigger escape. When she saw us, she broke down, and fell to the floor. And there, just, just behind her, was our son. Seven at the time, just staring at me. I felt sick.

(Pause.)

DAVE. I'll go in if it helps you, Kate. *(Pause.)* Em... I, eh, I tried to kill myself. I was bleeding out of it. I was at a party and there were bags of coke everywhere, literally everywhere. Sarah went home and I stayed on it, I always would. I'd say it was three or four days later, I went home. I cleared out my whole bank account over those few days. On coke, pills, mdma, everything really. *(Pause.)* Sarah lost it when I got home, obviously. We fought, she was trying to talk to me and I pushed her. Didn't mean to, but I did. She fell and I just ran. I don't even know why I ran but I did. *(Pause.)* The route I took and most of it, jaysus, is pretty hazy but I was found later that day, with two broken legs. Jumped into The Liffey. Tide was out and I smacked off the bottom. I just remember wanting to silence it all. My mind, my body, my life.

(Pause.)

CHRISTINE. I'll keep mine brief, if I can. I was found in the schoolyard of my daughter's primary school. Don't remember how I got there but it was a Monday morning. There I was, lying on the ground. All the children arriving for school, their parents with them. The principal knew me and pulled me into the school. She gave me a cup of coffee to sober me up and asked me what had happened. As if she didn't know. If I didn't know her, I'd say the guards would have been called. That was… that my was lowest. I felt like a piece of shit. Passed out, in my daughter's old school.

> *(There's a long pause.* **KATE** *has her head down.)*

STEPHEN. Are you being completely honest with yourself, Kate?

> *(Pause. Lights down.)*

Scene Fourteen

(14th July. The Lakelands Centre, Dublin. The same set up as before, maybe people are in different seats.)

DAMIEN. Ah, I bleeding lied, didn't I? I know why I did it.

(Slight pause.)

Course I do.

(Slight pause.)

I came through the group the first time and was doing well. Was starting to think I could, you know, meet someone. Have a little happiness. Figured it wasn't too much to ask. I hurt a lot of people. People I love. My son doesn't even talk to me. Ex-wife hates me. But I've tried, really tried. To get better, you know?

(Slight pause.)

I met someone. Natalie. Beautiful. French.

DAVE. You speak French?

DAMIEN. Jaysus, no. Can barely speak English. She lives around the corner from me. We'd see each other from time to time. Here and there. Around the area. Share a smile, a passing glance. Did I like her? Yeah. Was I afraid? Terrified. But I got up the courage and I asked her to dinner. Expecting her to fully shoot me out of the sky, man. But, but she agreed. Strangely, because you should see this woman.

DAVE. Gorgeous?

DAMIEN. Beautiful. Smart. Funny.

DAVE. Triple threat.

DAMIEN. A major triple threat, man. *(Pause.)* Well, we went out, had a great time. Lovely dinner, amazing company. Laughed all night, it was, it was really nice. It was truly the nicest evening I'd had. In a very long time. Like you said before, Dave. You feel, like, like you don't deserve it, almost. Like you're not worthy of something that... that pure, pure of heart, because she is. I don't know much about that sort of thing but her, Natalie, she's one of the good ones. *(Pause.)* After, I was like a school kid, man. Full of beans. Excited, happy. We walked, talked and I dropped her home.

(Slight pause.)

DAVE. That all sounds alright.

DAMIEN. Were you not listening, man? It was more than alright. But, eh, but at her door, she... she, eh, she kissed me.

DAVE. Go on, Damien.

DAMIEN. No, not. "Go on, Damien." That's not good for anyone. *(Pause.)* I panicked... turned and walked away. I said nothing. Didn't say goodnight or anything. It was like déjà vu. I saw it all. Everything I'd done. The sex with strangers. Sex with men, women, whoever, whenever. It all flooded my brain like the bursting of a dam.

(Pause.)

Familiar feelings that I thought were gone. I couldn't do that to Natalie. So, I got away. Walked, tried to clear my mind but I just couldn't shift those thoughts.

(Pause.)

Natalie, the kiss... I didn't stand a chance. Next thing I knew, I was in Players again. In the strip club and I was back to my old ways. Stayed all night and then a few of us left, went back to one of the girl's houses.

Like stepping into a time machine it was. Surrounded by drink, drugs, sex. For me, it was all about the latter. Me, two of the girls, a male friend of theirs. We, we just went at it all night.

(Pause.)

I woke up. Ashamed of myself and called Stephen that morning. I was doing so well and just, lost it, gone, back to... square one. *(Pause.)* Natalie, her bleedin' smile, man, that pure, fuckin'... pure beauty. How can something so good push me back to something so bad?

(Pause. Everyone completely understands the feeling.)

DAVE. It happens, man. You can give it another go.

DAMIEN. You don't get it, Dave. I ran from Natalie and ended up... in... in an orgy. Back to where I was before. Makes you feel helpless.

DAVE. I understand what you mean.

DAMIEN. Youngfella, you don't.

DAVE. I do/

DAMIEN. Dave/

DAVE. Some days it can get to me too and/

DAMIEN. You talk to Sarah?

DAVE. Yeah/

DAMIEN. That's my point. You stay away from drugs and you can still have someone. Someone who you can be close to. Who can I have?

(Pause.)

I don't want to be alone anymore. I don't want to be lonely. I want to love. I want to be loved, you know?

But I'm afraid. Afraid to get close to someone. Afraid to be intimate because… look what I do to them.

(Lights down.)

Scene Fifteen

(Lights up. 28th July. The Lakelands Centre, Dublin. The same set up as before, maybe people are in different seats.)

DAVE. Ah, shite.

CHRISTINE. Shite? It's a good thing, you eejit.

DAVE. You know what I meant.

DAMIEN. I think what these two are trying to say is that we'll miss you, Rebecca.

REBECCA. I'm going to miss you too. All of you.

CHRISTINE. Even Dave?

DAVE. Piss off.

REBECCA. Even Dave.

STEPHEN. You're ready to stand on your own two feet.

REBECCA. Sure about that?

STEPHEN. Would I lie to you?

REBECCA. Hmmm...

STEPHEN. With how you've approached your recovery. Helping yourself, helping me, helping the group. I'm proud of you.

REBECCA. Thanks, Stephen. You've been great.

STEPHEN. It was all you.

DAVE. I'm not able for this.

REBECCA. Would you stop. I'm not dying.

DAVE. Still.

REBECCA. You've got Damien here to look after you.

DAVE. That's reassuring.

REBECCA. We'll still be in touch.

KATE. Thanks, Rebecca. You've helped me a lot over the past few months.

REBECCA. As you have helped me.

DAVE. Fuck, I'm going to miss you.

    (Lights down.)

Scene Sixteen

(Lights up. 4th August. The Lakelands Centre, Dublin. The same set up as before, maybe people are in different seats.)

STEPHEN. I know, I know but we know this happens. People come and people go. One day, you lot will go too.

DAMIEN. Been there.

STEPHEN. That's our aim. Each of you will be exactly like Rebecca.

DAMIEN. You'd miss her around the place.

CHRISTINE. You would, she was very calming.

DAVE. Yeah, that fed into the group. I liked that energy, man.

KATE. She made me feel so welcome.

DAMIEN. And we didn't?

KATE. You did. She just helped me a lot in her last few months. Encouraged me to talk.

STEPHEN. She had that influence. *(Pause.)* Kate, last week you spoke about your family, I'd like to come back to that.

KATE. Now?

STEPHEN. Yes. Tell me about your family.

KATE. Well, there's not too much to tell. There was me, my nanny, my mam and my dad. My nanny died, then he left and it was us. Me and her. That's my family.

My folks didn't really give a shit. We all just kind of floated along, you know?

STEPHEN. That must have been lonely?

(Pause.)

KATE. Incredibly lonely.

(Pause.)

My dad was gone and my mam was just working away. I continued to work in the bar, continued to drink. Before, during and after work. Don't think I was ever sober in that bar.

(Pause.)

Just spiralled. Until I got to…rock bottom. My real rock bottom.

(Slight pause.)

One night, my mam came into the bar and asked me to drive her car home. She had a date. Well for her. I couldn't tell her I was drinking so I said yes. I wasn't going to drive it, I'd leave it there.

*(Slight pause. **STEPHEN** is sitting forward in his chair.)*

A few of us drank most of the night. Until everyone started to leave, so I left too. They were all waiting for a taxi and I thought, I've the car there. Come on, I'll drop everyone home. They all refused, and hopped in their taxis. I was a little pissed off with them so I said I'd grab my own but/

STEPHEN. You didn't drive the car, did you?

*(**STEPHEN** glances towards **CHRISTINE**, who is listening intently.)*

KATE. I did.

CHRISTINE. You got behind the wheel. Locked?

*(**STEPHEN** immediately cuts in.)*

STEPHEN. Let me stop you there, Kate.

*(Pause. **CHRISTINE** remains calm.)*

CHRISTINE. You were drunk and you drove?

STEPHEN. Okay.

CHRISTINE. Why would you do that?

STEPHEN. Christine.

KATE. What's going on?

*(**STEPHEN** stands up and walks **CHRISTINE** from the room.)*

CHRISTINE. *(Leaving.)* You're disgusting, how could you do that?

STEPHEN. Come on, Christine. Wait outside and let me deal with this.

CHRISTINE. A safe space, Stephen. This shouldn't be happening!

(They leave.)

KATE. *(Turning to the others.)* What's happening?

(Pause.)

DAVE. Christine's daughter was killed by a drunk driver.

(Slight pause.)

KATE. What?

DAVE. Yeah. I mean, you shouldn't be in the same group together.

*(Pause. **KATE** begins to hyperventilate. **STEPHEN** re-enters.)*

DAMIEN. It wasn't you, Kate.

DAVE. It's okay, breath.

DAMIEN. It wasn't you, Kate.

DAVE. It wasn't you.

> *(**KATE** starts to cry, uncontrollably. Everyone looks at her. After a few moments **DAVE** goes to comfort her.)*

STEPHEN. Don't do that. There's no physical contact in group. She has to deal with this herself.

> *(They all sit as she continues. Some watch, others look away.)*

> *(Lights down.)*

Scene Seventeen

(Lights up. 11th August. The Lakelands Centre, Dublin. The same set up as before, maybe people are in different seats.)

STEPHEN. I'd like to apologise to you both and the group, what happened last week should never have happened. We're here now though, and we've agreed that taking one of you out will do more harm than good. We can use this, to heal and move on.

(Pause.)

KATE. This was my fault. When I was in treatment I wasn't exactly honest, I held back. A lot. I never spoke about the accident. My ma left and wanted nothing to do with my rehab. So there was nobody to tell them the truth, only me and I wasn't ready for that. I was ashamed. I'm so sorry, Christine.

CHRISTINE. I know you are. It wasn't you that took my daughter.

KATE. It could have been.

CHRISTINE. It could have been, but it wasn't. I was thinking about you all week. I'm so sorry, Kate.

(Pause.)

KATE. I need to know that my actions have consequences.

(Lights down.)

Scene Eighteen

(Lights up. 25th August. The Lakelands Centre, Dublin. The same set up as before, maybe people are in different seats.)

DAVE. It's the fucking baby, man.

STEPHEN. The baby?

DAVE. The baby. My baby.

STEPHEN. We've spoken about this before, Dave. You need to slow down.

DAMIEN. Yeah, you're not making any sense, kid.

DAVE. Okay. Right, sorry. I'm just a little off today.

STEPHEN. Okay, there we go. You're feeling off. What happened this week?

DAVE. So, so the other day. Sarah asked me for a chat. To talk. About us.

STEPHEN. To talk about your relationship?

DAVE. To talk about the three of us. Me, her, the baby.

STEPHEN. Okay. Well, it's a conversation that needs to happen, Dave.

DAVE. I know but it brought up so much.

STEPHEN. What did it bring up?

DAVE. It brought up the past. The stuff I've done, you know? She said it's made it all real for her.

STEPHEN. It's made it all real for her?

DAVE. Yeah, like if I relapse. What'll happen?

STEPHEN. So, she's worried about you?

DAVE. She knows I've been doing well but that doesn't stop her worrying, you know? She's afraid. What if it does happen?

STEPHEN. It's not going to happen.

DAVE. She's worried about the fact that I'm in control of it and nobody else, you know?

STEPHEN. She can help too.

DAVE. I know and come on, you all know how much she helps. But the baby has her stressed. It won't just be the two of us anymore. And if I relapse now she's left with a baby, on her own, because she can't go through it all again. She can't help me like she did before. So if I go, I go alone.

STEPHEN. You're not going to go, Dave. You're stronger than that.

DAVE. The pressure of that though. I said it before, it's okay fucking up my own life but I can't do that to my baby's.

STEPHEN. And you won't.

DAVE. What if I do?

DAMIEN. Youngfella, look at me. You're not going to mess it up. Look how well you're doing. We told you, use this as motivation.

DAVE. She brought up loads, Damien.

DAMIEN. What do you mean?

DAVE. She told me that she knew. Knew it all. The stuff I used to do when I was out of it. Hiding it from her, thinking she didn't notice but she did. She even knew I took Casey's money. The story I told her, about someone breaking in. She saw right through it.

DAMIEN. Why didn't she tell you before?

DAVE. She thought it would push me over the edge, she was afraid of how I'd react. I was unpredictable. And what if that unpredictability comes back?

STEPHEN. It's good that she's talking about all of this, Dave.

DAVE. I know but she said her life can't be about recovery anymore. I go to meetings three times a week and she needs to know that I'm okay because her attention can't be on that anymore. We were a team, and now I've to do it alone.

DAMIEN. You don't have to do it alone.

STEPHEN. Exactly, we're here.

DAMIEN. All of us.

STEPHEN. And just know that Sarah will be too. She's just trying to focus on your baby.

DAVE. I know. It's just that so much is changing and I don't want to fall, you know?

>   *(Pause.)*

Everything with the baby. Then there's the celebrations. The fucking celebrations.

>   *(Lights down.)*

Scene Nineteen

(Lights up. 1st September. The Lakelands Centre, Dublin. The same as before. Everyone stands in a circle holding hands. Everyone is present except for **CHRISTINE.***)*

ALL. God, grant me the serenity to accept the things I cannot change,

Courage to change the things I can,

And wisdom to know the difference.

(They all then shake hands and say, "Keep coming back." to each other as they do.)

(Lights down.)

Scene Twenty

(Lights up. 8th September. The Lakelands Centre, Dublin. The same set up as before, maybe people are in different seats. Everyone is present except for **CHRISTINE**.*)*

DAVE. As long as you've known Christine, how many sessions has she missed?

(Pause.)

STEPHEN. None.

KATE. He has a point, Stephen.

DAVE. She's been a bit off the last while. She hasn't seemed herself.

STEPHEN. She hasn't been off. How great was it for her a couple of weeks ago?

DAVE. What?

STEPHEN. She apologised to everyone. To you, Kate. She said that everything has been clicking together. That she needs to remember her daughter. Find the good in that and celebrate her life.

DAVE. That was ages ago.

STEPHEN. That was an incredible breakthrough for her. So everyone just stay positive and don't let your mind go to that place.

KATE. This is my fault, isn't it?

STEPHEN. Nothing is wrong, there's an explanation/

DAVE. There is and it's not going to be good.

STEPHEN. Would you stop, we don't know that.

DAVE. You don't know either. First Michael and now Christine.

DAMIEN. Dave, we don't know if she's gone back out. So you panicking isn't going to help anyone. So let's calm down, yeah?

(*Pause.*)

And if she has. That is not your fault either, Kate. What happened here a couple of weeks ago is not the reason. It's something else.

STEPHEN. Thanks, Damien.

(*Pause.*)

DAVE. I'm sorry. You know I respect the two of you but I can't get my hopes up for them to be ripped apart again.

DAMIEN. Dave/

DAVE. No, man/

STEPHEN. Come on/

DAVE. This place is supposed to help me and this, this is not helping me!

STEPHEN. We don't know anything yet/

DAVE. Exactly and we need to. We need to know. We deserve to know.

STEPHEN. Calm down/

DAVE. I can't leave here and go about my week with this hanging over my head.

STEPHEN. Please/

DAVE. Fuck this!

(**DAVE** *pushes his chair to the ground and storms out of the session. Pause.*)

KATE. I'm with Dave on this. We need to know.

(*Pause.*)

(*Lights down.*)

Scene Twenty One

(Lights up. 15th September. The Lakelands Centre, Dublin. **STEPHEN** *is setting up the seats.* **REBECCA** *enters.)*

REBECCA. How are you?

STEPHEN. Ah jaysus, would you look who it is. Hello, stranger.

(They hug.)

REBECCA. Hugging an' all now.

STEPHEN. The joys of leaving group.

REBECCA. Fucking joys of it.

(They both laugh.)

I'm here to see Eamonn, he wanted a chat about something.

STEPHEN. About facilitating.

REBECCA. Yeah. How did you/

STEPHEN. Who do you think recommended you?

REBECCA. Ah, Stephen. That's... thank you.

STEPHEN. I knew you'd be interested. Also, who better, you know?

REBECCA. That means a lot.

STEPHEN. Don't mention it. How's everything been?

REBECCA. Really good, doing well.

STEPHEN. How's the family?

REBECCA. They're brilliant, I've been spending a lot of time with them. Swimming/

STEPHEN. You and your bleedin' swimming.

(They both laugh.)

REBECCA. I know. I did harp on about it a lot in the end, didn't I?

STEPHEN. All for good reason.

REBECCA. All for good reason.

(Pause.)

And how's everyone?

(Pause.)

STEPHEN. Em, it's been a rough couple of weeks.

REBECCA. Is everyone okay?

(Pause.)

STEPHEN. They miss you.

REBECCA. I miss them too, they're a great bunch.

STEPHEN. They are, they really are.

(Pause.)

Hopefully we can get them all to where you are.

REBECCA. With you on the case? No problem.

(Pause.)

And are you okay?

STEPHEN. Me?

REBECCA. Yeah. It was only after I left that I thought about it. We never actually asked were you okay.

STEPHEN. That's the gig.

REBECCA. I know, it just popped into my head.

(Pause. They both smile.)

So, are you doing okay?

(Pause.)

STEPHEN. We have good days and we have bad days. All of us.

(Lights down.)

Scene Twenty Two

(Lights up. 15th September. The Lakelands Centre, Dublin. The same set up as before, maybe people are in different seats. Everyone is present.)

STEPHEN. So, Christine. I just want to start by saying that we're so glad to have you back with us.

(Pause.)

We know it's been a tough couple of weeks. But you're here, we got you back and we're so happy that you are.

DAVE. You're one of us, Christine. I was thinking the worst.

(Pause.)

It's really great to see you. You had us all worried sick. We thought you were gone. Didn't we, Damien?

DAMIEN. We did.

STEPHEN. You mean a lot to this group, Christine.

KATE. It means the world to me that you're okay.

DAMIEN. It takes a lot to walk back in here. I know that all too well.

(Pause.)

STEPHEN. You didn't go to the bottom. You fell at a hurdle, but you're back. You were strong enough to walk back through that door and get help.

(Pause.)

So, how are you feeling, Christine? Do you want to tell us what happened?

(Pause.)

CHRISTINE. Em, firstly I just want to say that this is nobody's fault. Nobody in this room caused this.

(Pause.)

I'm crippled with shame even saying this but I'm pregnant.

(Pause.)

STEPHEN. You're pregnant?

CHRISTINE. Yeah, I'm eight weeks.

(Pause.)

DAVE. Congratulations, Christine. I'm fucking delighted/

STEPHEN. Stop, Dave. This isn't the time for that. This isn't good for your recovery, Chris/

CHRISTINE. I thought it was.

STEPHEN. What?

(Slight pause.)

You thought it was?

(Slight pause.)

Tell me you didn't plan this, Christine?

(Slight pause.)

CHRISTINE. Yeah.

STEPHEN. With who?

(Pause.)

CHRISTINE. Mark's his name. He's my brother's friend and he's always liked me, you know? So a little while back I invited him over and hoped that it would happen.

(Pause.)

STEPHEN. Why, Christine?

CHRISTINE. The last few months I've been seeing how happy Dave is. And a part of me thought, why do you get to be happy and I don't? I'm here every week, I'm trying so hard and nothing's working. So I thought, maybe that's why I'm not doing well. Maybe that's what I'm missing. A baby. That's why I'm like this in the first place, because I lost her.

(*Pause.*)

I couldn't have been more wrong.

STEPHEN. Did you tell Mark about this?

CHRISTINE. I did.

STEPHEN. Did you tell him that you planned it?

CHRISTINE. I did.

STEPHEN. Okay, at least you were honest with him. What did he say?

CHRISTINE. He went ballistic. As you'd expect. Screaming at me and it was only then that the weight of what I did hit me. When I saw the disbelief in his eyes. You could see his eyes thinking, "How the fuck could somebody do this?" I fucking lied to him. Told him I was protected, that we were protected and I knew full well that we weren't. Who fucking does that?

(*Slight pause.*)

He trusted me and I didn't care.

(*Slight pause.*)

I'm just so lonely and I just wanted the baby. Like it was before.

STEPHEN. If you're lonely, Christine. Get a dog. This is another life and you're only learning to care for yourself.

CHRISTINE. Maybe I shouldn't have told him anything.

STEPHEN. No, you made the right decision.

CHRISTINE. I really don't think I did. Just before he left he said that I was the most disgusting human being that he'd ever met. That I trapped him.

(Pause.)

STEPHEN. Is that what led to you drinking again?

(Slight pause.)

CHRISTINE. The night I found out I was pregnant I was thinking about it all. And for the first time in so long, I forgot about her. About Chloe and I was overcome with this... this guilt. Like I was replacing her with this... other baby... so I went and I took out the old photo albums.

(Pause.)

Every picture in that album is us. Her dad was never involved and I never wanted him to be. It was always just the two of us. I was looking through them and reliving it all. Every moment. The highs, the lows and everything in between.

(Pause.)

I haven't looked at those pictures in so long, I haven't been able to and now... I'm forgetting her. When I looked at them, I was so ashamed of myself. Forgetting her... then what I did to Mark. How could I do that to him? These are all the thoughts that are flying around my head as I look at fucking... photographs. I just know I won't love this baby as much as I loved her. How horrible is that?

STEPHEN. It's not horrible.

CHRISTINE. And what if the baby looks like her? How hard will that be? She's dead and I feel like I'm replacing her. So I started to overload with pictures and memories of her. It was like Damien said, it flooded my brain. Too much, too fast and I panicked. I really panicked.

(Slight pause.)

I left the house, walked to the shop and… I bought a bottle of vodka.

(Slight pause.)

I walked straight home, opened it up and drank it all. Every single drop.

(Slight pause.)

Until I passed out.

(Slight pause.)

I was only thinking of Chloe and how I've completely betrayed her.

(Slight pause.)

I really am the lowest of the low.

STEPHEN. You're not, Christine. We always say, no big life events during recovery but you're here, you're talking about it and we can help. It's not your fault.

(Slight pause.)

CHRISTINE. You think that isn't my fault? Look how you're all looking at me. You're as ashamed as I am.

(Slight pause.)

STEPHEN. Honestly, I don't think you're ready to be a mother again.

DAMIEN. That isn't helping right now, Stephen.

STEPHEN. You're not ready, Christine.

KATE. Can we come back to this?

DAVE. Yeah, she needs a break.

STEPHEN. No, this is too big not to talk about. Do you think you're ready to be a mother again, Christine?

    (Lights down.)

Scene Twenty Three

(Lights up. 6th October. The Lakelands Centre, Dublin. A session has just ended, **STEPHEN** *sits with his head in his hands. After a few moments,* **REBECCA** *pops her head in.)*

REBECCA. Stephen?

(Pause.)

Stephen?

(Pause. **STEPHEN** *slowly sits up.)*

STEPHEN. Hey, Rebecca. Sorry, in a world of my own there.

REBECCA. Tough session?

STEPHEN. No, not at all. Just didn't sleep too well last night.

(Pause.)

REBECCA. Are you sure everything's okay?

STEPHEN. Yeah, I'm grand. I'm just taking a second.

(Pause.)

Are you in to meet Eamonn again?

REBECCA. Yeah.

STEPHEN. How's it going?

REBECCA. Good. Just following the steps of it all.

STEPHEN. Yeah, it's just run of the mill assessments.

REBECCA. Just making sure I'm ready.

STEPHEN. It takes time to become a facilitator but you're well on the way.

REBECCA. I am.

> *(Slight pause.)*

Did something happen?

STEPHEN. Nothing's happened.

> *(Pause.)*

> *(Lights down.)*

Scene Twenty Four

(Lights up. 20th October. The Lakelands Centre, Dublin. The same set up as before, maybe people are in different seats.)

DAMIEN. Of course I worry. I have a lot of worries.

STEPHEN. Such as?

(Pause.)

DAMIEN. I worry about my son. What'll he think of me? Will he grow up hating me? Or know that I'm trying to change, for him.

(Pause.)

I worry about being alone. Spending the rest of my life unable to connect. To find someone, my equal, my counterpoint.

(Pause.)

They keep me up at night. Sometimes my heart feels like it's falling away, unused and rotting in my chest. And when I die, they'll cut me open and there'll be nothing there.

(Pause.)

I've this inherent fear that I'm becoming my father. He didn't love anything. Not me, not my mother. He loved absolutely nothing.

(Pause.)

Just fucking batterin' us, you know? Now, that he loved. Me, my mother, shit, he would beat us daily. Sometimes for something we did, sometimes for something we didn't.

(Pause.)

A grown man laying into a child half his size. My ma was a small woman, and fuck, it really aged her before her years, you know? As I got older, I used to... I'd piss him off so he'd come after me and leave her alone. I could take it.

(Pause.)

He'd leave me on the floor, face cut to bits. He'd go to bed and ma would go with him. She had to go, if she didn't, she'd get it even worse than I did. But as she would pass me, she'd blow me a kiss. Her way of saying, thanks for getting in the way, son.

(Pause.)

It was years of this. Until one night. He hit me, I hit him back and he bleedin' felt it. His eyes opened like he had seen a ghost. I didn't lick it off a stone.

(Pause.)

So, he threw me out. I tried to get ma to come with me, I couldn't leave her there with him. Without me, she'd have nobody to take the beatings but she wouldn't. She refused. She pushed me from the house.

(Pause.)

I think she wanted me away from there. She was a great woman, my mother. She lasted through all those beatings and outlived that bastard.

(Pause.)

I guess the fear I have, is that my son will talk about me, exactly how I just talked about him.

(Pause.)

STEPHEN. You never know.

DAVE. You never know? No, Damien.

KATE. You're not like him.

DAVE. You're going to be in his life. And fuck me, he's going to love you!

STEPHEN. Yeah.

DAVE. What's up with you, man?

STEPHEN. Nothing's up with me.

DAVE. You were the same with Christine a few weeks ago. The man's pouring his heart out and that's your response.

STEPHEN. Oh no, you clearly took me up wrong.

DAVE. Did I now?

STEPHEN. Yeah, what I meant was that we don't know. We can never know how others will perceive us.

(Pause.)

Like Damien. My daughter might have the same idea about me.

(Lights down.)

Scene Twenty Five

(Lights up. 3rd November. The Lakelands Centre, Dublin. The same set up as before, maybe people are in different seats.)

CHRISTINE. The scan went well. I, eh, I met Mark afterwards. We talked.

STEPHEN. How did that go?

CHRISTINE. He hates me and I don't blame him.

STEPHEN. It's still very raw for him, I'm sure.

CHRISTINE. He's right to hate me.

(Slight pause.)

He knows it's my choice to keep it. He needs to think if he wants to be in the baby's life but he's made it clear he wants nothing to do with me, he can barely even look at me.

STEPHEN. It'll be a challenge but you can do it.

CHRISTINE. The baby is bringing enough challenges to mind.

STEPHEN. Like what?

CHRISTINE. Chloe's school, for one, you know?

STEPHEN. Her school?

CHRISTINE. Yeah. I know it's down the line but that's the local school and I think about it all the time.

STEPHEN. And how you can't go back there?

CHRISTINE. Yeah and it has me thinking about Chloe more and more. Little things. Like, when she used to always insist on walking to school. Always. I'd ask if she wanted me to drive but she always insisted on walking.

(Pause.)

Always with the walking. Even when it was lashing, I'd have to drag her to the car. She was a head strong little divil.

(Pause.)

Sometimes I think if she didn't love walking so much, she'd still be here, you know? If she was a lazy little one. Or what if I was more assertive? Told her no and put her in the car. I know that's stupid to think but that's what goes through my head.

(Pause.)

That's what I think about. If only I did this differently or that, then maybe she'd be here. Maybe she'd still be waking me up in the morning, with that big happy head on her. If we didn't walk, the car would have come up on that path and we wouldn't have been there. We'd be safe. She'd be safe. I'd be me again and I wouldn't be here.

STEPHEN. Bollocks, Christine. Why are you here?

CHRISTINE. I've told you.

STEPHEN. Can I ask you a question, Christine. Do you believe you're an alcoholic?

CHRISTINE. Yeah

(Lights down.)

Scene Twenty Six

(Lights up. 24th November. The Lakelands Centre, Dublin. The same set up as before, maybe people are in different seats.)

KATE. I knew all along he was doing it, my ma did too. She became obsessed with it. Focused all of her energy on it.

STEPHEN. Did your father not tell her?

KATE. He just kept on denying it. She had no proof. She was going off what other people had told her.

STEPHEN. So he wasn't cheating on her then?

(Pause.)

KATE. It came out that he was. For years he was doing it. A woman he knew from work. That tore my mother apart. That's why she was never there for me, she was trying to fix that.

(Pause.)

He left eventually and then it was the two of us. She never tried with me. It was like when he left, he took her heart with him.

(Pause.)

That or she locked it up and threw away the key because I never saw it.

STEPHEN. Do you blame your alcoholism on your mother?

KATE. Fuck... if she just loved me. The way my nanny did? I got a taste of love for eight years of my life and then it was snatched from me. If she just hugged me, you know? Maybe the bottle wouldn't have been so comforting. It loved me more than my mother did and... and I love it more than I love her.

(Lights down.)

Scene Twenty Seven

(Lights up. 15th December. The Lakelands Centre, Dublin. After a session. **REBECCA** *and* **STEPHEN**.*)*

STEPHEN. It's just Christmas, that's all. And the stress of it.

REBECCA. Christmas, just Christmas?

STEPHEN. Yeah.

REBECCA. I've seen you around the place the last few months. We've talked.

STEPHEN. And?

REBECCA. You seem a bit distracted.

STEPHEN. Christmas does that to people, Rebecca. The shops, buying presents... families.

REBECCA. How is everything with your family?

STEPHEN. What?

REBECCA. Your family. Has there been any contact?

(Pause.)

STEPHEN. What kind of question is that?

REBECCA. You said you're buying presents. So, I thought one might have been for Michaela.

(Slight pause.)

STEPHEN. I always buy her a present. Every year.

REBECCA. Do you get to give them to her?

(Slight pause.)

STEPHEN. Not always but, eh, this year will be different.

REBECCA. Could be, yeah. She's old enough now. She might hear you out.

STEPHEN. Em... yeah.

REBECCA. So, is that what's affecting you?

STEPHEN. What, no, I'm just tired. Been busy sorting a few things in the house. The boiler burst a few weeks back and it's caused carnage.

> *(Pause.)*

What?

REBECCA. I think you're lying to yourself?

STEPHEN. I'm not.

REBECCA. That sounds like a load of shite, Stephen.

STEPHEN. Excuse me?

REBECCA. If someone was doing this in group, you'd recognise the signs a mile off. You're holding something in.

STEPHEN. I let everything out a long time ago.

REBECCA. Maybe you did, but sometimes that pain can come back.

STEPHEN. I'm not in any pain.

REBECCA. Recovery never stops, Stephen. Never. You know that and I know that.

STEPHEN. Recovery is my life.

REBECCA. Well then you need to tune in.

STEPHEN. Tune in?

REBECCA. Yes. To yourself.

STEPHEN. A facilitator now, are you?

REBECCA. Working on it, yes.

STEPHEN. So now I've to listen. You're going to help me, are you?

REBECCA. If you were in aftercare I'd recognise these signs. The whole group would.

STEPHEN. The stress of Christmas, that is all.

REBECCA. So you're going to keep on that story?

STEPHEN. As human beings it's okay to feel shit at times.

REBECCA. Shit isn't a feeling, Stephen.

STEPHEN. Listen to me. I don't need to talk and if I did, Rebecca. I wouldn't choose you to listen.

REBECCA. Go on, then. Ignore what's happening to you because I won't.

STEPHEN. Don't you say a fucking word.

REBECCA. About what? Thought nothing was wrong?

STEPHEN. Don't do that.

REBECCA. I won't say a thing but you need to listen to me and listen closely. You're struggling. You can see it. I can see it. I can feel it off you.

(**STEPHEN** *goes to leave.*)

Walking away won't solve anything, Stephen!

(*Lights down.*)

Scene Twenty Eight

(Lights up. 5th January. The Lakelands Centre, Dublin. The same set up as before, maybe people are in different seats.)

DAVE. She left me.

KATE. What?

CHRISTINE. What happened, Dave?

DAVE. She left me. She fucking left me.

(DAVE is freaking out.)

DAMIEN. You going to hop in here, Stephen?

STEPHEN. Yeah. What happened?

DAVE. A huge fucking fight, man. Huge.

STEPHEN. Was it your fault?

DAVE. What? No. It wasn't or... at least I don't think it was. We were talking about the baby and she said that she doesn't think she can leave it alone with me, when it comes, you know?

CHRISTINE. She said that?

DAVE. Yeah, she said I'm too volatile. I can do this, you know? It's the only positive thing I have in my life.

CHRISTINE. It was just a fight, it'll all be okay.

DAVE. You're pregnant, Christine. You'd trust me to be a good da, wouldn't you?

CHRISTINE. Of course. I think you'll make a great da.

DAVE. You do?

CHRISTINE. She'll come back.

DAVE. But... she took her things and went to her ma's.

KATE. That can happen after a fight, she'll come back.

DAVE. And what if she doesn't?

KATE. She will.

DAVE. You don't know that. None of you know that.

(DAVE stands up. So does STEPHEN.)

STEPHEN. Dave, it's okay. It's true, none of us know what's around the corner. She may leave you, she may not. This is just life. Bad things happen and there's nothing we can do about it. Nothing.

KATE. Em… not the most encouraging words, Stephen.

STEPHEN. Encouragement can only get us so far.

DAMIEN. Don't listen to him, Dave. She'll come back.

(DAVE walks to his seat. STEPHEN remains standing.)

STEPHEN. I'm not saying she won't come back but… she might not.

DAVE. I'll get her back.

STEPHEN. That's the spirit. You do that.

CHRISTINE. Are you okay, Stephen?

STEPHEN. Me? I'm absolutely fine.

CHRISTINE. You don't seem yourself.

STEPHEN. I'm just telling Dave what he needs to hear. I thought I'd get my family back if I got clean. I did that and look, I'm alone. So I feel it's my duty to prepare him for the possibilities. You need to accept that.

DAMIEN. You should be preparing him with a positive mindset.

(Pause.)

Then I walked away.

(Pause. Silence.)

DAVE. For fuck's sake, Damien.

DAMIEN. Excuse me?

DAVE. Why'd you do that?

DAMIEN. It was for the best.

DAVE. That's bollocks. You deserve to be happy. This woman, Natalie, she can make you happy.

CHRISTINE. I think your reason is valid, Damien.

KATE. Yeah, you're protecting her.

DAVE. What the fuck do you two know?

STEPHEN. Dave!

DAVE. You too, you couldn't give a shite about us the last while.

STEPHEN. Calm down.

DAMIEN. Youngfella, it's alright to be upset. You're going through a lot.

DAVE. I sit here and tell you what happened to me. And you do this?

DAMIEN. Two completely different situations.

DAVE. They're the exact same situation. You're just not man enough to take the chance!

DAMIEN. Now, watch your mouth!

DAVE. Sarah's left me. The best thing in my life. Gone, who knows what'll happen. I'm fucking devastated, man. And you turn your back and walk away from Natalie?

DAMIEN. It was for the best.

DAVE. Do you know how lucky you are? You've a woman that actually wants to be with you.

DAMIEN. You'll never understand.

DAVE. I do understand.

DAMIEN. You haven't a clue.

DAVE. What, are you afraid?

(DAMIEN stands.)

DAMIEN. I'm fucking terrified! Is that what you want to hear? Terrified!

DAVE. You're a coward!

(DAMIEN punches DAVE across the face.)

DAMIEN. I told you to watch your mouth!

(STEPHEN doesn't move, he just drops his head into his hands.)

(Lights down.)

Scene Twenty Nine

(Lights up. 5th January. The Lakelands Centre, Dublin. **STEPHEN** *sits, head in his hands as last seen.* **REBECCA** *speaks with him.)*

REBECCA. Eamonn wants to talk about what happened.

(Pause. **STEPHEN** *doesn't move.)*

STEPHEN. I can't believe he punched him. I'm losing control, Rebecca.

REBECCA. Did something happen over Christmas?

(Pause.)

You really don't look well, Stephen.

STEPHEN. I don't feel well. I'm just, tired. Really, really tired.

REBECCA. Maybe you need to take some time off. Go away, get some distance.

STEPHEN. How's everything with you?

REBECCA. Stephen, come on.

STEPHEN. I just want to know how you are.

REBECCA. I'm fine. I'm doing well.

STEPHEN. You'll be a facilitator before you know it. A good one too.

(Slight pause.)

I'm sorry. Before Christmas, I was out of order.

REBECCA. You know how to deflect better than most.

STEPHEN. This past year, it's just seems… *(Slight pause.)* Tried to visit my daughter on Christmas Eve. To give her a present. She answered the door and… threw it back in my face.

(Slight pause.)

I was just trying to see her more, talk to her more but… she still doesn't want anything to do with me. Then my ex-wife's new partner asked me to leave.

(Pause.)

Asked me to leave my own house. I bought that house.

(Pause.)

Standing in that garden, I could hear them.

(Pause.)

REBECCA. I think you need to step back, Stephen.

(Lights down.)

Scene Thirty

(Lights up. 15th January. The Lakelands Centre, Dublin. The same set up as before, maybe people are in different seats.)

(They all sit, **STEPHEN** *hasn't arrived yet.)*

DAVE. Where's he?

DAMIEN. He'll be here in a few.

CHRISTINE. Yeah, have some patience.

DAVE. I have loads of patience.

(Pause.)

KATE. This is kind of nice, in a strange way.

CHRISTINE. We can talk to each other?

KATE. Yeah. I feel like we never get to just chat as human beings.

CHRISTINE. Yeah, we never just get to talk about shite.

KATE. Exactly. Like a free class in school, isn't it?

CHRISTINE. I used to love free classes. Got any cards?

KATE. Few games of switch?

CHRISTINE. Jaysus, remember switch. I was unreal at switch.

KATE. Likewise. Jack back an' all that.

CHRISTINE. Was switch invented back in your day, Damien?

DAMIEN. Very funny.

CHRISTINE. Any more stories about the nephew?

DAMIEN. That mad bastard. He's gone to Pat's.

KATE. They locked him up?

DAMIEN. Ah, let's be honest. The youngfella was mental.

(They laugh.)

CHRISTINE. You're very quiet, not like you, Dave.

KATE. Not a fan of cards?

DAVE. Card games give me headaches.

KATE. Not surprised.

(Slight pause.)

DAVE. Here, I watched this film called *Jaws* last night.

KATE. Random.

DAVE. As you said, we never get to just talk. We always have to be on, don't we?

DAMIEN. What did you think?

DAVE. Of *Jaws*? Ah, man. It's a masterpiece. There wasn't a shot out of place. And that Richard Dreyfuss fella? He has some career ahead of him.

(Pause.)

DAMIEN. *Jaws* was made in the seventies, you gobshite.

DAVE. Fuck off!

CHRISTINE. Yeah, it's a pretty old film.

KATE. Haven't seen it.

DAVE. Aw, watch it! And after hearing how old it is, makes me love it even more. Masterpiece.

DAMIEN. It is.

DAVE. Here, is Richard Dreyfuss still alive?

DAMIEN. I think so.

DAVE. Thank God. That would've ruined my day.

DAMIEN. And he's had a very good career.

DAVE. I well believe it. He's unreal!

DAMIEN. Pretty sure he's an Oscar winner.

DAVE. Of course he is. There's nothing Dreyfuss can't do.

(Pause. The group just sits for a moment.)

Here, I wanted to save this but he's late. Myself and Sarah are back together.

(They all cheer.)

DAMIEN. Go on, son.

KATE. That's brilliant news.

CHRISTINE. She took you back. Didn't we say?

DAVE. You did. She's about ready to pop so maybe that scared her a little.

CHRISTINE. That's understandable.

(Slight pause.)

DAMIEN. That's really great news, youngfella.

DAVE. Thanks, Damien. Listen, I wanted to say it in front of the group as well. I'm sorry about what I said.

DAMIEN. It's okay.

DAVE. It's not, I was bang out of order.

DAMIEN. It's okay. I've been thinking a lot about what you said.

DAVE. You have?

DAMIEN. Yeah and what people don't really understand about my addiction/

*(Pause. **REBECCA** enters.)*

KATE. Rebecca!

CHRISTINE. What?

DAMIEN. Would you look at this.

CHRISTINE. What's going on?

KATE. What do we owe the pleasure?

REBECCA. Eamonn asked me to come in. Not sure how to say this but, I've a bit of housekeeping. It's Stephen.

> *(Sound suddenly dominates the scene. Dialogue from previous scenes begin to play and overlap as the scene continues. The following dialogue will not be heard.)*

DAVE. Is he okay?

KATE. What happened, Rebecca?

CHRISTINE. Where is he?

REBECCA. He was found in his home.

DAVE. Fuck/

KATE. Jesus Christ/

DAMIEN. Found in his home? Found, how?

> *(Slight pause.)*

REBECCA. He's overdosed.

DAVE. He's overdosed?

KATE. Is he okay?

DAMIEN. Is he alive?

> *(Slight pause.)*

REBECCA. He's dead.

DAVE. That can't be the truth/

REBECCA. It's the truth/

DAVE. It can't be.

REBECCA. It's the truth, Dave. I'm so sorry to be the one to tell you all this. Stephen is dead.

KATE. How did this happen?

CHRISTINE. He's been sober for so long/

DAMIEN. Jesus Christ/

CHRISTINE. Fucking hell/

DAVE. I can't believe he's dead/

DAMIEN. Do you know anything else at all?

REBECCA. We don't know what led Stephen to this point but I'm sure they'll want to speak with us… all of us.

(Blackout.)

The End

ABOUT THE AUTHOR

Lee is a writer based in Dublin. He is a founding member and Artistic Director of contemporary theatre company Bitter Like A Lemon.

He was one of six writers selected for the 2018 New Playwrights Programme to mark the Lyric Theatre Belfast's 50th year celebrations. He was a participant in Six In The Attic in 2018-2019, an Irish Theatre Institute initiative to support and promote emerging creative talent. He was also a participant in the prestigious Rough Magic SEEDS programme in 2016-2017.

Lee's play *In Our Veins* - commissioned by Dublin Port Company - had a hugely successful run on the Peacock Stage at The Abbey Theatre in 2019. His debut play *Leper + Chip* has been performed to great acclaim at Theatre Upstairs, Project Arts Centre, Edinburgh Fringe Festival (nominated for the Broadway Baby 5 Star Award and the National Student Drama Award for Best Play) Electric Picnic, Lyric Theatre, Belfast and axis:Ballymun, Cork. It was also produced by Inis Nua Theatre Company in Philadelphia, USA. Other productions include *Peruvian Voodoo* (Theatre Upstairs); *Slice, The Thief* (Smock Alley, axis:Ballymun); *Murder of Crows* (Theatre Upstairs, Project Arts Centre, Garter Lane, Lyric Theatre Belfast); *From All Sides* (Dublin Fringe Festival); The radio play *The Matron* as a part of *Dead Air* (Bram Stoker Festival); *The Tenements* (Collaborations, Smock Alley) and *24 Hour Plays* (Abbey Theatre). In 2020 *Leper + Chip* and *Slice, The Thief* were adapted for film as a part of Dublin Port Company's The Pumphouse Presents: alongside axis:Ballymun, Anu and Fishamble.

Lee was recently awarded an Arts Council Commission Award to write his new play *The Fortune Brothers* for axis:Ballymun. He is currently developing his first feature film, *J1: An American Odyssey*.

www.ingramcontent.com/pod-product-compliance
Ingram Content Group UK Ltd.
Pitfield, Milton Keynes, MK11 3LW, UK
UKHW021839210426
5322IPUK00022B/378